· VOICES · IN · POETRY ·

LANGSTON HUGHES | S. L. BERRY

CREATIVE EDUCATION

FOREWORD

No name is more synonymous with jazz poetry of the 1920s and '30s than Langston Hughes (1902–67). The Harlem Renaissance, also known as the "New Negro Movement," included a number of emerging poets and writers, such as Zora Neale Hurston, Claude McKay, and Countee Cullen, but Hughes established a reputation for originality and racial pride the equal of any writer.

Hughes grew up in an abolitionist family in a series of small midwestern towns. His father left the family, moving first to Cuba and then to Mexico. Raised in turn by his mother, grandmother, and family friends, young Langston experienced a rather lonesome childhood, which infused much of his most notable poetry.

All great poets lay claim to a few memorable lines or phrases. Instantly recognizable are Hughes's "a dream deferred," "black like me," "a raisin in the sun," and "I've known rivers." In his shorter poems, his diction, form, and rhythm are most closely akin to blues and jazz. As one reviewer put it, "he heard America jiving."

Unashamedly black at a time when being black was considered by many to be a misfortune, Hughes celebrated his African American identity and infused it with dignity. He sought to portray black working-class life realistically through its joys and struggles.

Hughes's great signature poem, "The Negro Speaks of Rivers," appeared in his first book of poetry, *The Weary Blues* (1926), which reviewers found stunning for its beauty, strength, and power. Although some writers, such as James Baldwin, considered Hughes's poetic achievement weak, Langston ignored the critics and soldiered on.

He may not have appealed to the literary lions, who searched in vain for complexity and militancy in his work, but the average black person loved Langston Hughes precisely because of his profound simplicity. His stature in the American canon today seems more secure than any poet of his generation. And yet his lasting literary achievement may be as a heroic exemplar for the many black American writers who followed him.

– J. Patrick Lewis, United States Children's Poet Laureate (2011-13)

I, TOO

I, too, sing America.

I am the darker brother.
They send me to eat in the kitchen
When company comes,
But I laugh,
And eat well,
And grow strong.

Tomorrow,
I'll be at the table
When company comes.
Nobody'll dare
Say to me,
"Eat in the kitchen,"
Then.

Besides,
They'll see how beautiful I am
And be ashamed—

I, too, am America.

From *The Weary Blues*

"My seeking has been to explain and illuminate the Negro condition in America and obliquely that of all humankind."

When Langston Hughes wrote this statement in 1967, he was explaining what he had tried to do over the course of his long writing career. His explanation also reveals why he was one of the 20th century's most respected and controversial writers.

Consciously setting out to write for and about black Americans, Hughes created a body of work—poetry, fiction, journalism, essays, plays, and song lyrics—that both chronicled the black experience and enlightened white Americans about racial issues. While decrying racism and the inequities it created for blacks and other minorities, Hughes called for cooperation among all races. In doing so, he crossed color barriers to gain widespread popularity.

His personal compassion, social awareness, and literary talent made him one of the most significant American writers in history.

Langston Hughes

NEGRO

I am a Negro:
  Black as the night is black,
  Black like the depths of my Africa.

I've been a slave:
  Caesar told me to keep his door-steps clean.
  I brushed the boots of Washington.

I've been a worker:
  Under my hand the pyramids arose.
  I made mortar for the Woolworth Building.

I've been a singer:
  All the way from Africa to Georgia
  I carried my sorrow songs.
  I made ragtime.

I've been a victim:
  The Belgians cut off my hands in the Congo.
  They lynch me still in Mississippi.

I am a Negro:
  Black as the night is black,
  Black like the depths of my Africa.

From The Weary Blues

CHILDHOOD

James Langston Hughes was born in Joplin, Missouri, on February 1, 1902, the only child of James and Carrie Hughes to survive infancy. Another son born two years earlier had died.

Carrie's family had been active abolitionists. A lover of books and plays, she had once dreamed of becoming a professional actress. Instead, like so many black women of her time, she had to settle for the jobs she could find, working as a stenographer and a waitress.

James Hughes wasn't able to pursue his professional goals, either. Hardworking and ambitious, he earned a law degree, but frustrated by limited opportunities in the United States, he left the country before his son was two years old. Though he periodically sent money, he never again lived with his family.

Langston and his mother moved to Lawrence, Kansas, and Langston lived with his grandmother as his mother moved from town to town in search of a decent job. Langston's grandmother often rented out every room in her house to boarders. When money was especially tight, she and her grandson lived on salt pork and wild dandelions, and Langston dressed in made-over clothes.

Langston suffered not only from poverty but also from restrictions that came with living in a segregated community. While he attended an integrated school, he wasn't permitted to take part in its team sports; neither could he join the Boy Scouts or swim at the YMCA. And suddenly one day his favorite movie theater put a sign in its box office window: No Colored Admitted.

In spite of these obstacles, Langston developed a natural sense of self-confidence, thanks in large part to his grandmother. One-quarter Cherokee, Mary Langston had always lived as a free woman and insisted that all people had the right to be free. Under her influence, Langston learned to endure the hardships of prejudice without surrendering his dignity or pride.

Carrie Hughes and her son Langston, 1902

Children, I come back today

To tell you a story of the long dark way

That I had to climb, that I had to know

In order that the race might live and grow.

Look at my face—dark as the night—

Yet shining like the sun with love's true light.

I am the child they stole from the sand

Three hundred years ago in Africa's land.

I am the dark girl who crossed the wide sea

Carrying in my body the seed of the free.

I am the woman who worked in the field

Bringing the cotton and the corn to yield.

I am the one who labored as a slave,

Beaten and mistreated for the work that I gave—

Children sold away from me, husband sold, too.

No safety, no love, no respect was I due.

Three hundred years in the deepest South:

But God put a song and a prayer in my mouth.

God put a dream like steel in my soul.

Now, through my children, I'm reaching the goal.

Now, through my children, young and free,

I realize the blessings denied to me.

I couldn't read then. I couldn't write.

I had nothing, back there in the night.

Sometimes, the valley was filled with tears,

But I kept trudging on through the lonely years.

Sometimes, the road was hot with sun,
But I had to keep on till my work was done:
I had to keep on! No stopping for me—
I was the seed of the coming Free.
I nourished the dream that nothing could smother
Deep in my breast—the Negro mother.
I had only hope then, but now through you,
Dark ones of today, my dreams must come true:
All you dark children in the world out there
Remember my sweat, my pain, my despair.
Remember my years, heavy with sorrow—
And make of those years a torch for tomorrow.
Make of my past a road to the light
Out of the darkness, the ignorance, the night.
Lift high my banner out of the dust.
Stand like free men supporting my trust.
Believe in the right, let none push you back.
Remember the whip and the slaver's track.
Remember how the strong in struggle and strife
Still bar you the way, and deny you life—
But march ever forward, breaking down bars.
Look ever upward at the sun and the stars.
Oh, my dark children, may my dreams and my prayers
Impel you forever up the great stairs—
For I will be with you till no white brother
Dares keep down the children of the Negro mother.

From *The Negro Mother and Other Dramatic Recitations*

EDUCATION

When Langston was 12 years old, his grandmother died, and he went to live with some family friends. When he was 13, his mother finally sent for him to join her in Lincoln, Illinois, where he found he had a new family. Having divorced his father, Langston's mother had married Homer Clark, who had an infant son. Langston was delighted. "I liked my stepfather a great deal," he later wrote in his autobiography, *The Big Sea*, "and my baby brother, also; for I had been very lonesome growing up all by myself."

Academically and socially, Langston did well in Lincoln. One teacher remembered him as handsome and intellectually advanced. When his 8th-grade classmates elected him class poet, Langston wrote a 16-verse poem celebrating the school. He read his poem aloud at graduation ceremonies, and he was so elated at the applause he received that he decided then and there to continue writing poetry.

The summer before he started high school, Langston and his family moved to Cleveland, Ohio.

The four years he spent at Cleveland's Central High School proved invaluable to his development both as a poet and as a person. Though the school was predominantly white—Hughes was 1 of only 10 black students in his class—racial problems were rare. Most of the students were from families that had only recently immigrated to the U.S., and they tended to be more racially tolerant than many other white Americans.

Central High School provided Langston with more than a textbook education. He was a member of the student council and the French club, served as editor of the yearbook, and ran on the school's championship track team. He was also involved in politics, a passionate interest for many of the foreign-born students and their families. Langston got his first exposure to socialist and communist ideologies from his white friends. This early introduction to radical politics had a tremendous impact on his development as a writer and social activist.

Langston with friends at Central High School, c. 1919

WHEN SUE WEARS RED

When Susanna Jones wears red
Her face is like an ancient cameo
Turned brown by the ages.

Come with a blast of trumpets,
        Jesus!

When Susanna Jones wears red
A queen from some time-dead Egyptian night

Walks once again.

Blow trumpets, Jesus!

And the beauty of Susanna Jones in red
Burns in my heart a love-fire sharp like pain.

Sweet silver trumpets,
        Jesus!

From *The Weary Blues*

When he was a junior in high school, Langston received a letter from his father, the first in 11 years. James Hughes had become a successful businessman in Mexico. Now he wanted Langston to join him in Mexico for the summer.

Despite his mother's opposition—"Your father is a devil on wheels," she said—Langston was curious. "In my mind I pictured my father as a kind of strong, bronze cowboy, in a big Mexican hat," he wrote in *The Big Sea*, "going back and forth from his business in the city to his ranch in the mountains, free—in a land where there were no white folks to draw the color line."

But reality didn't match Langston's fantasy. Though he loved Mexico, he hated his father, a man so focused on making money that he had no time to enjoy life. The key source of friction between Langston and his father, however, was the latter's bigotry against his own race. "My father hated Negroes," wrote Hughes later. "I think he hated himself, too, for being a Negro. He disliked all of his family because they were Negroes and remained in the United States where none of them had a chance to be much of anything."

Despite his disdain for his father's way of life, Langston returned to Mexico following his graduation from high school in 1920. He wanted to go to college, and he needed his father's financial help to do so. Unable to agree with his father on a degree program—Langston wanted to study writing at Columbia University in New York City; his father wanted him to study engineering in Switzerland—Langston spent an entire year in Mexico. Miserable but productive, he wrote and published a number of poems. He also tutored wealthy Mexicans in English to earn enough money to go to New York.

Seeing his son's determination, Langston's father finally relented and agreed to help pay his tuition and living expenses at Columbia.

Scene on the road to Monterrey, Mexico

Rain

Thunder of the Rain God:
> And we three
> Smitten by beauty.

Thunder of the Rain God:
> And we three
> Weary, weary.

Thunder of the Rain God:
> And you, she, and I
> Waiting for nothingness.

Do you understand the stillness
> Of this house
> In Taos
Under the thunder of the Rain God?

(continued)

USA 20c
Ferocactus wislizeni
Barrel Cactus

Sun

That there should be a barren garden

About this house in Taos

Is not so strange,

But that there should be three barren hearts

In this one house in Taos—

Who carries ugly things to show the sun?

Moon

Did you ask for the beaten brass of the moon?

We can buy lovely things with money,

You, she, and I,

Yet you seek,

As though you could keep,

This unbought loveliness of moon.

Wind

Touch our bodies, wind.

Our bodies are separate, individual things.

Touch our bodies, wind,

But blow quickly

Through the red, white, yellow skins

Of our bodies

To the terrible snarl,

Not mine,

Not yours,

Not hers,

But all one snarl of souls.

Blow quickly, wind,

Before we run back

Into the windlessness—

With our bodies—

Into the windlessness

Of our house in Taos.

From *Selected Poems*

Langston's sojourn at Columbia University was short-lived. University officials were surprised to discover that the young man who had enrolled by mail from Mexico was actually black. They gave him the worst dormitory room on campus. When he volunteered to work for the student newspaper, he was given the job of covering fraternity events—all of which were closed to blacks.

Angered by the racism he had unexpectedly encountered and bored with his classes, Langston began to explore New York, going to Chinatown with a Chinese-American friend, and to Harlem on his own. "I spent as much time as I could in Harlem," Langston wrote of this time. "Everybody seemed to make me welcome. The sheer dark size of Harlem intrigued me."

By the end of his freshman year, Langston wanted nothing more to do with Columbia. He wrote to his father to tell him he was leaving the university, a move that marked the end of their relationship. From then until his death in 1934, James Hughes rarely communicated with his son. In fact, in his will he omitted all mention of Langston.

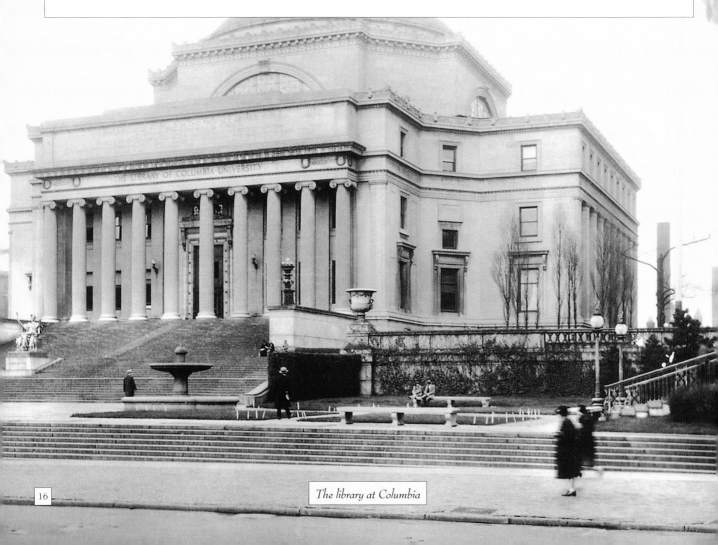

The library at Columbia

1754 - COLUMBIA UNIVERSITY - 1954

U. S. POSTAGE

3¢

MAN'S RIGHT TO KNOWLEDGE AND THE FREE USE THEREOF

THEME FOR ENGLISH B

The instructor said,

> *Go home and write*
> *a page tonight.*
> *And let that page come out of you—*
> *Then, it will be true.*

I wonder if it's that simple?
I am twenty-two, colored, born in Winston-Salem.
I went to school there, then Durham, then here
to this college on the hill above Harlem.

I am the only colored student in my class.
The steps from the hill lead down into Harlem,
through a park, then I cross St. Nicholas,
Eighth Avenue, Seventh, and I come to the Y,
the Harlem Branch Y, where I take the elevator
up to my room, sit down, and write this page:

It's not easy to know what is true for you or me
at twenty-two, my age. But I guess I'm what
I feel and see and hear, Harlem, I hear you:

(continued)

hear you, hear me—we two—you, me, talk on this page.

(I hear New York, too.) Me—who?

Well, I like to eat, sleep, drink, and be in love.

I like to work, read, learn, and understand life.

I like a pipe for a Christmas present,

or records—Bessie, bop, or Bach.

I guess being colored doesn't make me *not* like

the same things other folks like who are other races.

So will my page be colored that I write?

Being me, it will not be white.

But it will be

a part of you, instructor.

You are white—

yet a part of me, as I am a part of you.

That's American.

Sometimes perhaps you don't want to be a part of me.

Nor do I often want to be a part of you.

But we are, that's true!

As I learn from you,

I guess you learn from me—

although you're older—and white—

and somewhat more free.

This is my page for English B.

From *Montage of a Dream Deferred*

After leaving Columbia, Hughes worked first on a vegetable farm on the outskirts of New York City, then as a deliveryman for one of Manhattan's most exclusive floral shops. But he yearned to travel, so he applied for work on ships heading for foreign ports. "It seemed to me now that if I had to work for low wages at dull jobs, I might just as well see the world," Hughes wrote in *The Big Sea*. He got his chance when he signed on as a mess boy on a freighter bound for Africa.

For six months, the ship Hughes was on made its way up and down the western coast of Africa, loading and unloading cargo. Though he believed common ancestry bound him to other blacks throughout the world, Hughes was surprised to find that his copper-brown skin and wavy hair made him white in African eyes. At one point, when he asked if he could attend a ritual drumming ceremony, he was turned down because the tribal god would not permit a white man to be present.

Still, his time in Africa was inspirational, resulting in several poems condemning white colonialism or celebrating black unity and beauty. His racial pride eventually made his poetry popular among many Africans. Later in his life, he visited several African countries as an honored guest of groups interested in learning about black American culture.

Natives of Kenya at the river

AFRO-AMERICAN FRAGMENT

So long,
So far away
Is Africa.
Not even memories alive
Save those that history books create,
Save those that songs
Beat back into the blood—
Beat out of blood with words sad-sung
In strange un-Negro tongue—
So long,
So far away
Is Africa.

Subdued and time-lost
Are the drums—and yet
Through some vast mist of race
There comes this song
I do not understand,
This song of atavistic land,
Of bitter yearnings lost
Without a place—
So long,
So far away
Is Africa's
Dark face.

From *Dear Lovely Death*

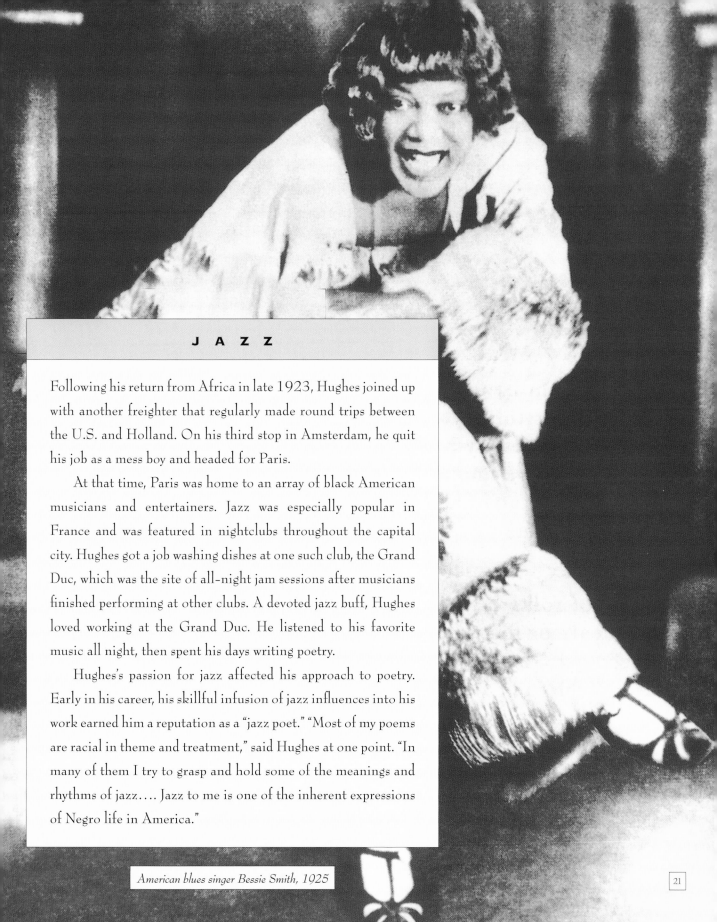

J A Z Z

Following his return from Africa in late 1923, Hughes joined up with another freighter that regularly made round trips between the U.S. and Holland. On his third stop in Amsterdam, he quit his job as a mess boy and headed for Paris.

At that time, Paris was home to an array of black American musicians and entertainers. Jazz was especially popular in France and was featured in nightclubs throughout the capital city. Hughes got a job washing dishes at one such club, the Grand Duc, which was the site of all-night jam sessions after musicians finished performing at other clubs. A devoted jazz buff, Hughes loved working at the Grand Duc. He listened to his favorite music all night, then spent his days writing poetry.

Hughes's passion for jazz affected his approach to poetry. Early in his career, his skillful infusion of jazz influences into his work earned him a reputation as a "jazz poet." "Most of my poems are racial in theme and treatment," said Hughes at one point. "In many of them I try to grasp and hold some of the meanings and rhythms of jazz…. Jazz to me is one of the inherent expressions of Negro life in America."

American blues singer Bessie Smith, 1925

TRUMPET PLAYER

*T*he Negro
With the trumpet at his lips
Has dark moons of weariness
Beneath his eyes
Where the smoldering memory
Of slave ships
Blazed to the crack of whips
About his thighs.

The Negro
With the trumpet at his lips
Has a head of vibrant hair
Tamed down,
Patent-leathered now
Until it gleams
Like jet—
Were jet a crown.

The music
From the trumpet at his lips
Is honey
Mixed with liquid fire.
The rhythm
From the trumpet at his lips

W.C. HANDY
Father of the Blues

Is ecstasy
Distilled from old desire—

Desire
That is longing for the moon
Where the moonlight's but a spotlight
In his eyes,
Desire
That is longing for the sea
Where the sea's a bar-glass
Sucker size.

The Negro
With the trumpet at his lips
Whose jacket
Has a fine one-button roll,
Does not know
Upon what riff the music slips
Its hypodermic needle
To his soul—

But softly
As the tune comes from his throat
Trouble
Mellows to a golden note.

From *Fields of Wonder*

Hughes's return to New York in 1924 signaled the beginning of his fame. Publishing his jazz-tinged poems in the NAACP's *Crisis* and the Urban League's *Opportunity*, as well as in *Vanity Fair* and *The New Republic*, Hughes became a key figure in the Harlem Renaissance. At its peak during the "Roaring Twenties," the Harlem Renaissance was a period of vitality for black writers and musicians, with artists such as Hughes, blues singer Bessie Smith, and jazz composer Duke Ellington becoming internationally known.

In 1926, Hughes's first book, *The Weary Blues*, was published to a chorus of praise from black and white reviewers alike. It was essentially a book about Harlem, inspired by Hughes's love of black music. One reviewer remarked that no other poet could write "as tenderly, understandingly, and humorously about life in Harlem."

The Weary Blues appeared as its 24-year-old author returned to college, this time at Lincoln University, an all-male, black institution located in the wooded countryside south of Philadelphia. Though well on his way to success as a writer, Hughes felt compelled to finish what he'd started at Columbia—the pursuit of a college degree. With financial help from a wealthy literary patron, Hughes spent three years at Lincoln, sandwiching his classwork between the demands of his mounting fame.

Though he produced very few new poems during his time at Lincoln, Hughes had enough existing work to compile a second book, *Fine Clothes to the Jew*, which was published in 1927. He also wrote one of his best-known essays, "The Negro Artist and the Racial Mountain." In it, Hughes argued against surrendering racial pride to the hope of acceptance by whites. The urge among some black artists to be "as little Negro and as much American as possible," wrote Hughes, was a "mountain standing in the way of any true Negro art."

Langston Hughes as a busboy, shortly before his career took off

THE WEARY BLUES

Droning a drowsy syncopated tune,
Rocking back and forth to a mellow croon,
    I heard a Negro play.
Down on Lenox Avenue the other night
By the pale dull pallor of an old gas light
    He did a lazy sway....
    He did a lazy sway....
To the tune o' those Weary Blues.
With his ebony hands on each ivory key
He made that poor piano moan with melody.
    O Blues!
Swaying to and fro on his rickety stool
He played that sad raggy tune like a musical fool.
    Sweet Blues!
Coming from a black man's soul.
    O Blues!
In a deep song voice with a melancholy tone
I heard that Negro sing, that old piano moan—

(continued)

"Ain't got nobody in all this world,

Ain't got nobody but ma self.

I's gwine to quit ma frownin'

And put ma troubles on the shelf."

Thump, thump, thump, went his foot on the floor.

He played a few chords then he sang some more—

"I got the Weary Blues

And I can't be satisfied.

Got the Weary Blues

And can't be satisfied—

I ain't happy no mo'

And I wish that I had died."

And far into the night he crooned that tune.

The stars went out and so did the moon.

The singer stopped playing and went to bed

While the Weary Blues echoed though his head.

He slept like a rock or a man that's dead.

From the collection *The Weary Blues*

POLITICS

With the onset of the Great Depression of the 1930s came the end of the Harlem Renaissance and the renewal of Hughes's radicalization. Since high school, he had been a supporter of radical causes, especially if they promised better living conditions for people of color. The miseries brought on by the Great Depression heightened his commitment to left-wing politics and strengthened his support for groups that called for fundamental change in America.

In 1931, Hughes went on a nine-month odyssey throughout the southern and southwestern U.S., doing readings at both black and white universities and colleges along the way. That trip reinforced his rancor against the Jim Crow laws then in effect throughout the South and left him dismayed at the lack of social activism among educated blacks.

The following year, Hughes went to the Soviet Union, where he toured several remote Central Asian republics and wrote about his experiences for Soviet newspapers and magazines. To examine how people were faring under Soviet rule, he visited farms, cotton mills, factories, schools, hospitals, and union halls, talking with workers and Communist Party leaders in large cities, small towns, and isolated rural settlements.

Hughes was pleased with much of what he learned, but though his travels reinforced his support for Soviet ideals, he never joined the Communist Party. "I did not believe that political directives could be applied to creative writing," he told a friend. Besides, on one crucial issue Hughes disagreed sharply with the Soviet Communists: They considered jazz to be decadent music. Jazz was an essential element of being black, asserted Hughes. "I wouldn't give up jazz for a world revolution," he said.

Some Depression-era African Americans had substandard homes

ONE MORE "S" IN THE U.S.A.

Put one more S in the U.S.A.
To make it Soviet.
One more S in the U.S.A.
Oh, we'll live to see it yet.
When the land belongs to the farmers
And the factories to the working men—
The U.S.A. when we take control
Will be the U.S.S.A. then.

Now across the water in Russia
They have a big U.S.S.R.
The fatherland of the Soviets—
But that is mighty far
From New York, or Texas, or California, too.
So listen, fellow workers,
This is what we have to do.

    Put one more S in the U.S.A. [Repeat chorus]

But we can't win out by just talking.
So let us take things in our hand.
Then down and way with the bosses' sway—
Hail Communistic land.
So stand up in battle and wave our flag on high,
And shout out fellow workers
Our new slogan to the sky:

    Put one more S in the U.S.A.

But we can't join hands strong together
So long as whites are lynching black,
So black and white in one union fight
And get on the right track.
By Texas, or Georgia, or Alabama led
Come together, fellow workers
Black and white can all be red:

    Put one more S in the U.S.A.

(continued)

ЗДРАВСТВУЕТ
ПОБЕДА
ГЛО-СОВЕТСКО-
МЕРИКАНСКОГО
ЕВОГО СОЮЗА!
СТАЛИН
ПОЧТА СССР
30
КОП.

Oh, the bankers they all are planning

For another great big war.

To make them rich from the workers' dead,

That's all that war is for.

So if you don't want to see bullets holding sway

Then come on, all you workers,

And join our fight today:

Put one more S in the U.S.A.

To make it Soviet.

One more S in the U.S.A.

Oh, we'll live to see it yet.

When the land belongs to the farmers

And the factories to the working men—

The U.S.A. when we take control

Will be the U.S.S.A. then.

Langston Hughes wrote this poem as a workers' song. It
was published in the *Daily Worker*, a Communist tabloid,
in 1934, but was never included in any of his books.

SOLITUDE

Although Hughes was interested in the lives of others, he himself was an extremely private man. "He was very likeable and easy to get on with," noted Hungarian writer Arthur Koestler, "but at the same time one felt an impenetrable, elusive remoteness which warded off all undue familiarity."

The one person who was able to penetrate Hughes's remoteness was a beautiful Chinese ballet dancer named Si-Lan Chen, whom he met in 1933 while staying in Moscow. Thirty-one years old at the time, Hughes was surprised to find himself in love. (Some scholars believe that Hughes may have been homosexual.) While it wasn't the first love affair he'd had, it was the most serious. But it ended when Hughes was unable to commit himself as fully to the relationship as Si-Lan wanted. A loner by nature, Hughes preferred the solitary activities of writing and traveling to the demands of a serious relationship.

Langston Hughes with a friend, Carolyn Clark, in 1933

*D*esire weaves its fantasy of dreams,
And all the world becomes a garden close
In which we wander, you and I together,
Believing in the symbol of the rose,
Believing only in the heart's bright flower—
Forgetting—flowers wither in an hour.

Published in the July 1930 issue
of the NAACP's magazine *Crisis*

Rose USA 18c

"Six months in one place is long enough to make one's life complicated," Hughes once remarked to a friend. Afflicted with wanderlust, Hughes loved to ramble. But when he returned to the U.S. from the Soviet Union in 1933, he wanted to settle down and write. At the insistence of his friend, wealthy white arts patron Noël Sullivan, Hughes accepted a one-year, rent-free stay at Sullivan's beach home in Carmel, California. There he wrote pieces that appeared in publications as diverse as *Esquire* and the American Communist Party's newspaper, the *Daily Worker*.

From Carmel, Hughes moved on to a variety of places over the next few years—Las Vegas, Los Angeles, Chicago. He also spent time in Mexico, where he went after receiving word of his father's death, and in Spain, where he covered the Spanish Civil War for the *Daily Worker*. Finally, in 1938, Hughes accepted an offer from his old friends Toy and Emerson Harper to share their Harlem apartment; in 1945, they went in together in buying a three-story Harlem townhouse. While he continued to travel extensively, Hughes lived with the Harpers for the rest of his life.

Harlem, 1936

MADAM'S PAST HISTORY

My name is Johnson—
Madam Alberta K.
The Madam stands for business.
I'm smart that way.

I had a
HAIR-DRESSING PARLOR
Before
The depression put
The prices lower.

Then I had a
BARBECUE STAND
Till I got mixed up
With a no-good man.

Cause I had a insurance
The WPA
Said, We can't use you
Wealthy that way.

I said,
DON'T WORRY 'BOUT ME!
Just like the song,
You WPA folks take care of yourself—
And I'll get along.

I do cooking,
Day's work, too!
Alberta K. Johnson—
Madam to you.

From *One Way Ticket*

RENUNCIATION

In the 1940s, Hughes became disillusioned with radical politics. For years he had scraped by financially, using the money he made from his writing to promote left-wing, anti-imperialist ideals. But as he got older, he tired of living hand-to-mouth; he began to actively seek commercial success. He sold short stories to mainstream magazines, wrote scripts for Hollywood movie studios, and composed opera librettos, Broadway show tunes, and popular songs. In short, he did whatever seemed creatively interesting and financially promising. His leftist friends criticized him for selling out.

But it was more than just a desire to make money that separated Hughes from radical politics. The Soviet Union's leader, Joseph Stalin, whom Hughes had once admired, signed a nonaggression pact with Nazi Germany's Adolf Hitler. Hughes was shocked by Stalin's willingness to sign any sort of agreement with Hitler, and his shock deepened when he learned that Stalin was purging the Soviet Union of "undesirables." Poles, Jews, and members of other ethnic groups were being imprisoned, tortured, and killed. In disgust over Stalin's actions, Hughes broke his ties with the communists.

Though he became less radical in some of his political beliefs, Hughes continued to call for an end to racism and segregation in America. He asserted that the only difference between life for Jews in Nazi Germany and life for blacks in the U.S. was that the latter had freedom of speech. "Democracy permits us the freedom of a hope, and some action towards the realization of that hope," he said. But the lack of opportunities for full participation in American political, business, and cultural life maintained a society in which "Negroes are secondary Americans." That was a role Hughes never accepted for himself, nor believed anyone of any race should have to endure.

Hughes at anti-communist hearings

PRIX NOBEL DE LA PA[IX]

POSTE AERIEN[NE]

MARTIN LUTHER KING - LUTTE CONTRE LE RACISME

GUILLAME

700ᶠ

REPUBLIQUE DU MALI

HARLEM

What happens to a dream deferred?

Does it dry up
like a raisin in the sun?
Or fester like a sore—
And then run?
Does it stink like rotten meat?
Or crust and sugar over—
like a syrupy sweet?

Maybe it just sags
like a heavy load.

Or does it explode?

From *Montage of a Dream Deferred*

DEFERRED

This year, maybe, do you think I can graduate?
I'm already two years late.
Dropped out six months when I was seven,
a year when I was eleven,
then got put back when we come North.
To get through high at twenty's kind of late—
But maybe this year I can graduate.

Maybe now I can have that white enamel stove
I dreamed about when we first fell in love
eighteen years ago.
But you know,
rooming and everything
then kids,
cold-water flat and all that.
But now my daughter's married
And my boy's most grown—
quit school to work—
and where we're moving
there ain't no stove—
Maybe I can buy that white enamel stove!

Me, I always did want to study French.
It don't make sense—
I'll never go to France,
but night schools teach French.
Now at last I've got a job
where I get off at five,
in time to wash and dress,
so, si'l-vous plait, I'll study French!

Someday,
I'm gonna buy two new suits
at once!

All I want is
one more bottle of gin.

All I want is to see
my furniture paid for.

All I want is a wife who will
work with me and not against me. Say,
baby, could you see your way clear?

(continued)

THE MUSIC OF AMERICA IS FREEDOM'S SYMPH[...]

USA 3[...]

AUTH. NON-
PROFIT ORG.

Heaven, heaven, is my home!
This world I'll leave behind
When I set my feet in glory
I'll have a throne for mine!

I want to pass the civil service.

I want a television set.

You know, as old as I am
I ain't never
owned a decent radio yet?

I'd like to take up Bach.

    Montage
    of a dream
    deferred.

Buddy, have you heard?

From *The Langston Hughes Reader*

CHANGES

With the onset of the Civil Rights and Black Power movements of the 1960s, Hughes finally witnessed the public display of racial pride and activism he had long advocated. Ironically, however, among many of the more militant black activists of the time, he was considered out of step. His gentlemanly demeanor and his friendships with wealthy white liberals made him suspect to those who were demanding radical change. Suddenly, Hughes was considered too conservative.

But Hughes had weathered decades of criticism of his political beliefs, and he remained largely undisturbed by the new charges being leveled against him. He spent the last 15 years of his life working on such significant projects as *A Pictorial History of the Negro in America* and *The Book of Negro Folklore*, as well as on a series of popular children's books that included *First Book of Negroes, Famous Negro Music Makers*, and *Famous Negro Heroes of America*. He also edited a number of black poetry anthologies and became a respected mentor for several emerging black writers.

In August 1963, some 200,000 people demonstrated in Washington, D.C., for equal rights for black Americans

DINNER GUEST: ME

I know I am
The Negro Problem
Being wined and dined,
Answering the usual questions
That come to white mind
Which seeks demurely
To probe in polite way
The why and wherewithal
Of darkness U.S.A.—
Wondering how things got this way
In current democratic night,
Murmuring gently
Over *fraises du bois*,
"I'm so ashamed of being white."

The lobster is delicious,
The wine divine,
And center of attention
At the damask table, mine
To be a Problem on
Park Avenue at eight
Is not so bad.
Solutions to the Problem,
Of course, wait.

From *The Panther and the Lash*

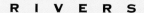

RIVERS

In May 1967, Langston Hughes checked himself into the New York Polyclinic Hospital, complaining of severe abdominal pains. Tests indicated he had a swollen prostate gland, and his physician recommended surgery. Hughes agreed to have the operation, and it went well.

The prognosis was for a complete recovery in a matter of days. However, three days after surgery, Hughes's temperature began to climb, his heart rate escalated, and he developed pneumonia. A postoperative infection had developed, and toxins began attacking his vital organs. On May 22, 1967, Hughes died at the age of 65.

A jazz trio played at his funeral, which was attended by nearly 300 writers, musicians, and black political leaders. Afterward, a group of Hughes's closest friends grasped hands and recited one of his best-known poems, "The Negro Speaks of Rivers." It was a moving tribute to the man who had inspired so many.

Langston Hughes, 1902–67

THE NEGRO SPEAKS OF RIVERS

I've known rivers:
I've known rivers ancient as the world and older than
the flow of human blood in human veins.

My soul has grown deep like the rivers.

I bathed in the Euphrates when dawns were young.
I built my hut near the Congo and it lulled me to sleep.
I looked upon the Nile and raised the pyramids above it.
I heard the singing of the Mississippi when Abe Lincoln
went down to New Orleans, and I've seen its
muddy bosom turn all golden in the sunset.

I've known rivers:
Ancient, dusky rivers.

My soul has grown deep like the rivers.

From *The Weary Blues*

ACKNOWLEDGMENTS

PHOTO CREDITS

The Beinecke Rare Book and Manuscript Library; The Bettmann Archive; Black Star (Griff Davis); Culver Pictures, Inc.; Magnum Photos (C. Capa, Ian Berry); Shutterstock (irisphoto1); Wide World Photos

Stamp designs © United States Postal Service. All rights reserved.

POETRY CREDITS

From *Selected Poems* by Langston Hughes. Copyright © 1947 by Langston Hughes. Reprinted by permission of Alfred A. Knopf, Inc. From *Selected Poems* by Langston Hughes. Copyright © 1959 by Langston Hughes. Reprinted by permission of Alfred A. Knopf, Inc. *Selected Poems* by Langston Hughes. Copyright © 1926 by Alfred A. Knopf, Inc. and renewed © 1954 by Langston Hughes. Reprinted by permission of the publisher. *Selected Poems* by Langston Hughes. Copyright © 1938 and renewed © 1966 by Langston Hughes. Copyright © 1959 by Langston Hughes. Reprinted by permission of Alfred A. Knopf, Inc.

SELECTED WORKS BY LANGSTON HUGHES

POETRY

The Weary Blues, 1926

Fine Clothes to the Jew, 1927

The Dream Keeper and Other Poems, 1932

Shakespeare in Harlem, 1942

Fields of Wonder, 1947

One Way Ticket, 1949

Montage of a Dream Deferred, 1951

Ask Your Mama: 12 Moods for Jazz, 1961

The Panther and the Lash, 1967

Black Misery, 1969

CHILDREN'S BOOKS

The First Book of Negroes, 1952

Famous American Negroes, 1954

The First Book of Rhythms, 1954

The First Book of Jazz, 1955

Famous Negro Music Makers, 1955

The First Book of the West Indies, 1956

A Pictorial History of the Negro in America (written with Milton Meltzer), 1956

Famous Negro Heroes of America, 1958

The First Book of Africa, 1960

PROSE

The Ways of White Folks, 1934

The Big Sea: An Autobiography, 1940

Laughing to Keep from Crying, 1952

The Best of Simple, 1961

Something in Common and Other Stories, 1963

OTHER WORKS

Five Plays by Langston Hughes, 1963

INDEX

Published by Creative Education

P.O. Box 227, Mankato, Minnesota 56002

Creative Education is an imprint of The Creative Company

www.thecreativecompany.us

Design by Stephanie Blumenthal

Production by The Design Lab

Art direction by Rita Marshall

Printed in the United States of America

Library of Congress Cataloging-in-Publication Data

Berry, S. L.

Langston Hughes / by S. L. Berry.

p. cm. — (Voices in Poetry)

Includes index.

Summary: An exploration of the life and work of 20th-century American
writer Langston Hughes, whose poetry is known for its accounts of the
African American experience and its call to racial equality.

ISBN 978-1-60818-327-2

1. Hughes, Langston, 1902–1967—Juvenile literature. 2. African American poets—
Biography—Juvenile literature. 3. Poets, American—20th century—Biography—Juvenile
literature. 4. Young adult poetry, American. I. Hughes, Langston, 1902–1967. II. Title.

PS3515.U274Z6172 2014

818'.5209—dc23   [B]   2013030156

CCSS: RL.4.1, 2, 3, 4, 5, 6; RL.5.2, 4, 6, 7; RI.5.1, 2, 3, 8

First Edition

9 8 7 6 5 4 3 2 1